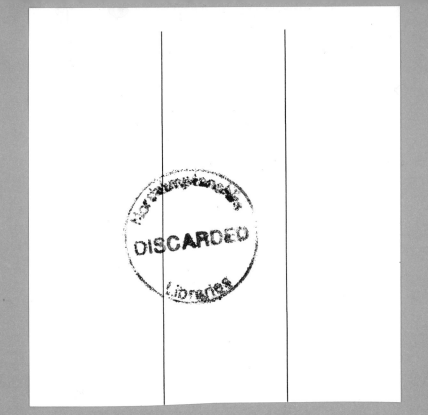

Northamptonshire

DISCARDED

Libraries

D0410383

INSPIRATIONAL LIVES

DAVID ATTENBOROUGH

NATURALIST VISIONARY

Sonya Newland

WAYLAND

First published in 2015 by Wayland

Copyright © Wayland 2015

Wayland
338 Euston Road
London NW1 3BH

Wayland Australia
Level 17/207 Kent Street
Sydney, NSW 2000

All rights reserved

Produced for Wayland by
White-Thomson Publishing Ltd
www.wtpub.co.uk
+44 (0)843 208 7460

Design: Tim Mayer (Mayer Media)
Proofreader: Izzi Howell

A catalogue record for this title is
available from the British Library.

ISBN: 978 0 7502 8569 8
ebook ISBN: 978 0 7502 9016 6

Dewey Number: 508'.092-dc23

Printed in China

Wayland is a division of Hachette
Children's Books, an Hachette UK
company.

www.hachette.co.uk

Picture acknowledgements:
The author and publisher would like
to thank the following for allowing
their pictures to be reproduced in
this publication.
Flickr: 29 (Johann Edwin Heupel/
Creative Commons License); **Getty
Images:** 10 (Popperfoto), 13, 15; **Nature
Picture Library:** 5 (Huw Cordey), 9
(Mike Salisbury), 11 (Ben Osborne), 19
(John Sparks), 20 (Peter Scoones), 22
(Ben Osborne), 24 (Mike Salisbury), 25
(Miles Barton), 27 (Neil Lucas), 28 (Neil
Lucas); **Rex Features:** 7 (Nick Cunard),
16 (David Sandison/The Independent);
Shutterstock: 8 (Baloncici), 12 (jaja), 18
(Brandon Alms), 21 (Monika Wieland),
23 (Paul Marcus), 26 (FloridaStock);
Thinkstock: 4 (Digital Vision), 17
(John Camemolia); **Wikimedia:** 6
(NotFromUtrecht/Creative Commons
License), 14.

Northamptonshire Libraries & Informaton Services BB	
Askews & Holts	

Contents

Life in the wild

Balanced on the edge of a small boat in the middle of the ocean, David Attenborough could barely contain his excitement. 'I can see its tail, just under my boat here,' he exclaimed. 'It's coming up ... it's coming up! There! The blue whale!' The enormous creature swam alongside the boat for a time, then dived downwards, its vast tail gracefully breaking the surface of the water before disappearing into the depths.

David and his crew were in the Pacific, filming his latest series for the BBC, *The Life of Mammals*. It was a stroke of luck to have caught this **endangered** animal on camera, and they were all excited. David was especially thrilled. In his seventies at the time, he had finally fulfilled a childhood dream – seeing with his own eyes the largest creature that has ever existed on earth.

TOP TIP

Being a naturalist is all about observing nature. Carry a notebook when you're out and about so you can sketch and make notes on the animals and plants you see, and where you see them. This will help you learn to pay attention to the details of the natural world.

In the programme, David explained that an animal as large as the blue whale could not survive on land, because the creature's bones would not be able to support its huge size.

Having spent more than half a century filming around the world, David has travelled further than any human in history apart from astronauts!

For The Life of Mammals, *David also got up close to a colony of meerkats in the Kalahari Desert.*

David has been lucky enough to enjoy many memorable moments like this. In his 60-year career as a naturalist and TV presenter, he has been to every corner of the globe. He has scaled mountains, descended into caves, climbed the world's tallest trees and navigated its most dangerous rivers.

On his travels, he has been bitten, stung, pecked, chased and charged at. Along the way, he has discovered new species and **pioneered** the latest filming techniques to reveal the natural world in ways it has never been seen before.

The Attenborough boys

David Attenborough was born in London on 8 May 1926. A few years later his parents, Frederick and Mary, moved to Leicester, where Frederick had been appointed head of the university. David and his two brothers grew up on the university **campus**. They were not a wealthy family, but the boys had a nanny to help look after them, as well as a cook and a maid.

David's childhood home, College House, is now part of the Maths Department at the University of Leicester.

The three Attenborough boys were very different from one another. The eldest, Richard, had little interest in studying – he longed to be a famous actor. David was the middle brother. He was the clever one, who worked hard at school and was fascinated by science and nature. The youngest, John, loved planes and cars. Because they all had such different interests, there was no rivalry between the boys and they got on well together.

WOW! David's younger brother John was obsessed with cars and later worked for the Italian car maker Alfa Romeo. In contrast, David says he 'can't bear motor cars' and he has never learnt to drive!

David's interest in nature started at an early age. As a young boy, he was a keen collector of fossils, rocks and birds' eggs, which he displayed in his own 'museum'. He also enjoyed roaming the grounds of the university, checking out the local wildlife. He would catch newts from a nearby pond and sell them to the **zoology** department to make some pocket money!

INSPIRATION

When David was seven, the archaeologist and writer Jacquetta Hawkes visited the Attenborough family. She admired his little museum and later sent him a box of fossils and other **artefacts** such as dried seahorses to add to his collection, encouraging his interest in natural history.

Richard Attenborough's dreams of becoming an actor and director came true. Despite their busy lives, he and David remained the best of friends until Richard's death in 2014.

Wartime studies

In 1939, when David was 13, the Second World War broke out. In August of that year, the male-dominated world the boys were used to changed for ever when two German Jewish girls came to stay with them.

Irene and Helga were brought to England as part of a government programme called Kindertransport, which helped Jewish children escape the dangers of **Nazi** Europe. Although the arrangement was meant to be temporary, the boys treated Irene and Helga as their sisters, and Frederick and Mary later adopted the girls.

INSPIRATION

David was greatly inspired by his father, whom the three boys called 'The Governor'. Because Frederick was a teacher, he drilled into his sons the importance of studying hard. He insisted that they win **scholarships** to prove they would be successful in their chosen careers.

There are memorials to the Kindertransport programme in both Britain and Germany. In all, around 10,000 Jewish children were helped by the programme.

The war raged for six long years. During this time, David finished his secondary schooling and won a scholarship to Cambridge University, where his father had taught before moving to Leicester. Unsurprisingly given his childhood passion, David chose to study natural sciences for his degree.

David probably never anticipated some of the situations his desire for adventure would lead him into! Here he is being filmed while dangling over the rainforest in Venezuela.

David enjoyed his time at Cambridge and his studies confirmed his love of zoology and **geology**. But life at university also made him realise that he didn't want to follow in his father's footsteps as a teacher and an academic. He wanted action and adventure.

The war ended in 1945, but young men still had to serve two years in the armed forces after they had finished their education. Once again, the three boys chose different paths – Richard joined the Royal Air Force, John went into the Army and David chose the Navy. He hoped that this might bring some of the excitement and international travel that he longed for, but his postings only took him as far as Scotland and Wales!

WOW!

During the war, David had a job in a factory making plastic buttons. He says it was the worst job he ever had!

Breaking into television

After leaving the Navy, David got a job editing science books for a children's publisher in London. But he soon realised that this was not the career path for him, and he began to look for other opportunities.

HONOURS BOARD

David is the only person in television history to have won a British Academy of Film and Television Award (BAFTA) for four different formats of TV programme: black and white, colour, high-definition (HD) and 3D.

Despite feeling dissatisfied at work, this was a joyful time for David in other ways. In 1950, he married Jane Oriel, whom he had met at university. The couple went on to have two children, Robert and Susan, and remained happily married until Jane's death in 1997. David was devastated by her sudden loss, but said he 'found **consolation** in the natural world'.

David at home with his wife, Jane, and his children. Robert now lives in Australia. Susan lives close to her father in London and sees him nearly every day.

In 1952, David finally got the job that would define the rest of his life – he was accepted as a trainee producer at the BBC. At the time, television was still quite new. There was only one channel in the UK, the BBC Television Service, and TV sets were considered a luxury item. David himself didn't even own a TV at the time!

David's first job at the BBC was in the TV Talks department, which produced all the channel's non-fiction programmes. One of his earliest responsibilities was producing the game show *Animal, Vegetable, Mineral?* On the programme, experts on art, history and archaeology tried to identify unusual artefacts. At last David was doing something that interested him!

The things David learnt in his early years at the BBC remain with him to this day. He understands that a successful programme relies on the skill and expertise of many different people – not just a good presenter.

WOW!

When David first joined the BBC, his boss, Mary Adams, told him that he shouldn't be a presenter because his teeth were too big! She soon changed her mind when she saw what a natural he was in front of the camera.

Animal encounters

The very first natural history programme David worked on was a series called *The Pattern of Animals*. It was also the first time he appeared on camera as a presenter. For the show, animals from London Zoo were brought into the BBC studio. There, David and the famous naturalist Julian Huxley would explain features such as their markings and courtship displays.

The Pattern of Animals gave David an idea for another TV show. He suggested that the BBC **collaborate** with London Zoo on an expedition to Sierra Leone in Africa. They would collect rare animals that would then be housed in the zoo. He wrote a memo to Mary Adams outlining his plan for this series, which would combine scenes from the wild with studio shots so viewers could see the animas in close-up.

WOW!

In 1961, David went to Kenya to make a short film about the lioness Elsa, who had been raised by humans. He woke from a nap one day to find the lioness asleep on top of him!

The Pattern of Animals *taught viewers about animal behaviour such as mating rituals. Much later, David experienced one of his favourite career moments when seeing the mating dance of the bird of paradise.*

David suggests that if you want to be a documentary film-maker, you should start by trying to make your own film. He says, 'It is very easy now. It wasn't in my time but these days home video is not all that expensive.' The subject of your video can be something small – a snail or a bird, perhaps. When you edit your film, try to tell a story with it. This will test your skills as both a naturalist and a film-maker.

For Zoo Quest, David worked closely with Jack Lester, the curator of London Zoo's reptile house. Here, the two men are planning a quest to British Guiana.

The idea of the show was to catch animals so they could be kept in **captivity**. This might seem shocking today, but attitudes towards animals were very different 50 years ago. People felt that it was acceptable to hunt or capture them. David later said he regretted the way some of the animals were treated.

Mary liked David's proposal and gave the show the go-ahead. *Zoo Quest* first appeared on television in 1954. It was hugely popular and the series eventually ran for nearly 10 years. It marked the start of David's adventures travelling to far-flung places to film unusual animals.

In charge at the BBC

By 1965, David had made such a mark at the BBC that he was made Controller of the company's new channel, BBC2. It was a great promotion for an ambitious man still in his thirties.

However, David loved all the travelling he had done on *Zoo Quest*. He wanted to make sure that this new job didn't mean he was stuck behind a desk all the time, so he asked for a **clause** in his contract that said he could still make his own TV programmes.

David's programme First Life, *in 2010, explained the origins of life on our planet and the beginnings of evolution – ideas that were first suggested by Charles Darwin.*

ON

THE ORIGIN OF SPECIES

BY MEANS OF NATURAL SELECTION,

OR THE

PRESERVATION OF FAVOURED RACES IN THE STRUGGLE FOR LIFE.

By CHARLES DARWIN, M.A.,

FELLOW OF THE ROYAL, GEOLOGICAL, LINNÆAN, ETC., SOCIETIES;
AUTHOR OF 'JOURNAL OF RESEARCHES DURING H. M. S. BEAGLE'S VOYAGE
ROUND THE WORLD.'

LONDON:
JOHN MURRAY, ALBEMARLE STREET.
1859.

The right of Translation is reserved.

INSPIRATION

David's favourite book is *On the Origin of Species* by Charles Darwin. It was very **controversial** when it was first published in 1859. In it, Darwin explains his theory of how species survive and **evolve** through a process called 'natural selection'. At the time, most people believed that God had created people and animals.

David set out on a mission to make BBC2 the most **diverse** and interesting channel on TV. He wanted people with all different interests to enjoy watching, so he **commissioned** programmes on travel and science, music and art. He was also in charge when the BBC moved from black and white to colour. He did so well in charge of BBC2 that in 1969 he was made Director of Programmes for the whole BBC.

WOW!

One of the programmes that David wrote and presented during this period was called *A Blank on the Map*. In it, he and his film crew travelled to a previously unexplored part of New Guinea. There, they came across a tribe of people who had never had contact with other humans before.

David celebrates his appointment as Controller of BBC2 in 1965.

However, David was desperate to be back out in the wild. He explained that the natural world was his 'greatest source of excitement' and what 'makes life worth living'. Although he had made a few programmes in this time, in 1972 he decided to quit his job as Director and return to writing and filming full time.

It was at this point that he began working on a series that would change documentary film-making for ever...

A day in the life of David Attenborough

David is now in his late eighties, so he does not spend as much time travelling and filming abroad as he used to. However, while most people of his age retired years ago, David still has a busy work schedule.

No two days are the same for David. He writes all his own scripts, so sometimes he spends the day writing at his home in Richmond, West London, while his daughter Susan helps around the house and makes sure he eats lunch!

TOP TIP

It takes a lot of patience to make documentaries about nature. Most animals are very shy of humans, so you have to wait a long time to see one. David says it is important to figure out at the start if you are the kind of person who can 'spend your time sitting in a tent waiting for a bird to do something'!

David spends his time at home writing scripts or books, or signing photographs and replying to letters from his fans.

Writing a script can take a long time. David always begins by drawing up a list of questions that he wants answered. He then talks to the programme's researchers, and together they assemble a mountain of notes to work out what each show in a series will cover! It is only after months of preparation that filming can begin.

David usually has several projects on the go, so while he's writing one show, he will be filming another. When he isn't writing, he can usually be found on location or in the studio recording programmes such as *Natural Curiosities* or his amazing 3D documentaries for Sky.

INSPIRATION

David has great respect for the film crews he travels with, admiring their skill and patience. 'People assume I do all the work,' he says. 'I keep having to tell them, it was the cameraman, not me.'

Natural Curiosities *investigates some of the world's weirdest creatures, including the duck-billed platypus, which David describes as having 'a beak like a bird and fur like a rabbit'.*

Life on Earth

In 1979, *Life on Earth* was broadcast in the UK. The series made David Attenborough a household name. Using the latest technology – and a lot of patience – David and his team captured some incredible **footage**. No one had ever seen animals in this way before!

For the series, David travelled all over the world to chart the evolution of life on our planet. He showed how life began in the seas. He described how the millions of different species developed – how they slowly spread across the land and took to the skies. The last episode explained how human life eventually began in Africa.

WOW!

Life on Earth was not only popular in Britain. Over 500 million people in nearly 100 countries around the world tuned in to see the ground-breaking documentary series.

The first episode of Life on Earth *included filming in the rainforests of South America, where unusual animals such as this red-eyed tree frog live.*

HONOURS BOARD

There are nine *Life* series
in total:
Life on Earth
The Living Planet
The Trials of Life
Life in the Freezer
The Private Life of Plants
The Life of Birds
The Life of Mammals
Life in the Undergrowth
Life in Cold Blood

One of David's favourite moments when filming *Life on Earth* was getting close to mountain gorillas in Rwanda, East Africa. While crawling through the thick **undergrowth**, David suddenly came across a female gorilla. Turning to the camera, he described, without a script, how human-like these apes are: 'Their sight, their hearing, their sense of smell are so similar to ours that they see the world in much the same way as we do.'

The series was a huge success. The public loved David's calm, intelligent presenting style. It wasn't long before the BBC asked if he would write another series, and in 1982 filming began on *The Living Planet*.

More than 35 years after his first encounter with mountain gorillas, David still campaigns to save these critically endangered animals through the International Gorilla Conservation Programme (IGCP).

Knight of the realm

The Living Planet was another huge success. David was a firm favourite with the viewing public and people started referring to him as a 'national treasure'. In 1985, he was invited to Buckingham Palace, where the queen awarded him a knighthood while his wife and daughter looked on proudly.

HONOURS BOARD

David can put seven titles after his name to show the honours he has received:

OM – Order of Merit

CH – Order of the Companions of Honour

CVO – Royal Victorian Order

CBE – Commander of the Order of the British Empire

FRS – Fellow of the Royal Society

FZS – Zoological Society of London

FSA – Society of Antiquaries of London

There was no time to relax and enjoy his success, though. The BBC had realised it had a winning formula in the *Life* series, and decided to make it a **trilogy**. The programme that was intended to complete the collection was called *The Trials of Life*. This time, David focused on animal behaviour and the different stages of their life cycles.

For The Trials of Life, *David wanted to film under water. He nearly drowned when practising in the hotel swimming pool after his 'bubble helmet' sprang a leak!*

While filming the series, David found himself in some unusual situations. One of the most memorable was being marched over by hundreds of red crabs while filming on a beach on Christmas Island, in the Indian Ocean. He said: 'The crabs just treated me as another obstacle – a particularly oddly shaped boulder, perhaps – and simply walked straight over.' Despite his fear of the sharp claws clambering over him, David managed to deliver his lines to camera like a professional.

WOW!

One of the most famous scenes from *The Trials of Life* shows a killer whale hunting and playing with its prey – a young sea lion – before killing it. This behaviour had never been filmed before.

Filming the killer whale was a risky shoot for the cameramen, who had to get into the water, close to the creature, to get their amazing footage.

From Antarctica to paradise

The BBC intended *Life* to end with the third series, but the shows had been a global **phenomenon** – and the public wanted more! So throughout the 1990s, David added three more series to the collection: *Life in the Freezer*, *The Private Life of Plants* and *The Life of Birds*.

WOW!

David always travels economy class on his flights abroad. If he is offered an upgrade, he will only accept if all his film crew are allowed to join him in business or first class.

David spent a lot of time among the penguins when filming Life in the Freezer. *The animals look cute, but David found the smell almost overpowering!*

Writing and presenting these series involved a huge amount of work and, of course, a great deal of travel. However, David welcomed the challenge. He was especially excited by the latest developments in film technology, which allowed him to capture plant and animal life in even more astonishing detail.

Life in the Freezer, a study of Antarctica, took three years to film. To get shots of the amazing creatures that have adapted to life in this harsh environment, the crew used several **innovative** techniques. To get underwater footage, for example, they found a way of mounting their cameras on special inflatables and operating them by remote control.

The *Life* series had largely focused on animal life, but now David decided to share his passion for plants. He was worried that the programme wouldn't be exciting enough to capture the public's interest, but once again film techniques came to the rescue. Using **time-lapse photography**, *The Private Life of Plants* uncovered the mysteries of plant life in stunning images.

Amazingly, in between these series for the BBC, David managed to make several shorter series for other channels, including *The First Eden*, *Lost Worlds*, *Vanished Lives* and *Attenborough in Paradise*.

WOW!

The corpse flower is the largest flower in the world and it blooms for just three days every seven years. David and his crew witnessed this rare event while filming *The Private Life of Plants* – one of the most special moments of his career.

The penguins weren't the only thing with a bad smell – the corpse flower is so-called because it smells like rotting flesh.

The end of *Life*

As the 2000s dawned, David – long past normal retirement age – showed no signs of slowing down. 2002's *The Life of Mammals* was his most epic undertaking yet. The series investigated why mammals, including humans, are the most successful creatures on earth.

The Life of Mammals was broadcast in the early days in digital television. After each episode, viewers who had a digital TV could take part in an interactive quiz hosted by David himself.

Although in his late seventies, David was still willing to get down in the mud to film a piece about butterfly migration for Life in the Undergrowth.

Filming once more took David all over the world, from the Arctic **tundra** to the baked landscapes of Tanzania, where early human ancestors originated. **Infrared** technology caught the nocturnal behaviour of big cats that had never been seen before. As always, viewers were wowed.

While *The Life of Mammals* gave David a personal encounter with the blue whale, the largest creature on earth, his next series, *Life in the Undergrowth*, took him into the world of some of the smallest known creatures – **invertebrates**. These creatures had rarely been filmed before because it was so difficult to catch them on camera. However, David's team used special lenses to catch every vibrant detail of creatures such as spiders, snails, bees and butterflies.

Looking back over the last 20 years, David realised that the *Life* programmes had covered almost every type of plant and animal. Only two major groups were left – reptiles and amphibians. And so he wrote *Life in Cold Blood*. Broadcast in 2008, this series completed an extraordinary collection of nature documentaries. 'The evolutionary history is finished,' David said. 'The **endeavour** is complete.'

INSPIRATION

When David was 12, one of his adopted sisters gave him a piece of amber with ancient creatures preserved in it. In 2004, this piece inspired David's programme *The Amber Time Machine*. A similar piece of amber was used in the blockbuster film *Jurassic Park*, which starred his brother Richard.

For Life in Cold Blood, *David went to the steaming volcanic Galapagos Islands to record the mating habits of giant tortoises.*

Life in 3D

HONOURS BOARD

David has several species of plants and animals named after him:

Attenborosaurus conybeari (a type of plesiosaur)

Materpiscis attenboroughi (an ancient fish)

Blakea attenboroughi (a flowering tree)

Nepenthes attenboroughii (a carnivorous pitcher plant)

Ctenocheloides attenboroughi (a type of shrimp)

Prethopalpus attenboroughi (a spider)

Zaglossus attenboroughi (an echidna)

In between writing and shooting the last two *Life* series, David kept himself busy with other projects. He **narrated** *Blue Planet*, a ground-breaking history of the world's oceans. He also narrated *Planet Earth* in 2006. For *Frozen Planet*, he not only provided some narration, but also appeared on camera and wrote one of the episodes.

David has always been keen to use the latest technology in his programmes. This interest has led him to help develop a new collection of documentaries for Sky's 3D channel.

In one of these shows, *Galapagos 3D*, David returned to the islands of the giant tortoise and met Lonesome George, the last known Pinta Island tortoise. Lonesome George died just two weeks later, and his species became **extinct**.

David wrote and presented an episode called 'On Thin Ice' for the series Frozen Planet. It was all about the effect that climate change and global warming are having on polar animals.

One of David's latest 3D projects brings the creatures housed in the Natural History Museum to life in three dimensions – from the **dodo** to dinosaurs. *Natural History Museum Alive* had a special screening at the museum itself, where celebrities and royalty joined David in putting on their 3D glasses to enjoy the show!

WOW!

In all his travels, the closest David has come to death is falling 35 metres from a cliff in the Lake District. And he wasn't even there filming a television programme – he was just climbing the cliff for fun!

David has travelled further and seen more natural wonders than almost anyone else in the world. But his curiosity and passion for nature is as strong as it was when he was a boy collecting fossils and catching newts. 'I just wish the world was twice as big and half of it was unexplored,' he says.

David had filmed at the Natural History Museum during The Life of Mammals, *using the huge blue whale skeleton housed there to bring the creature to life for viewers.*

The impact of David Attenborough

Throughout David's long career, he has been hugely influential. His early work in television set the high standards of broadcasting that the BBC still strives to achieve. But it is his work as a broadcaster and naturalist that has had the greatest impact.

David has spread his own passion for wildlife to people all over the world. Thanks to him, we know much more about the natural world – and the threats to it – than we ever did. And it's not just the public that David has educated. Some of the filming techniques he used showed scientists details about certain species that they had never known before!

Over the years, David has introduced people to some of nature's weirdest – and most wonderful – creations. This is a manatee, or sea cow.

WOW!

David says the species he would most like to take on his personal ark to save from extinction is the rare black lion tamarin – a monkey found only in São Paulo, Brazil.

HONOURS BOARD

David has written or co-written more than 25 books. These include six that accompanied the *Zoo Quest* series in the 1950s and 1960s, and those to go with the *Life* series. He has also written an autobiography: *Life on Air*.

Even after all the experiences he has had, David is still filled with wonder at the amazing beauty and diversity of nature.

He may have shown people the importance of protecting the animals that share our world, but David's desire for **conservation** goes beyond endangered species. He has increasingly spoken out about the dangers of **climate change** and how human behaviour is affecting our planet.

Having someone as greatly respected as David speaking out on such issues makes people sit up and take notice. As he points out: 'The natural world is in greater peril than ever ... and we're the only species that can do anything about it.'

David's plans for the future involve more campaigning on environmental issues as well as continuing his 3D documentaries. In 2014, he announced that he was planning a trip to Australia to introduce his 3D projects. No doubt he will also enjoy some time with his son Robert while he's there!

Bedtime

Goodnight!

reading

Playtime

watching TV

bathrobe

bubbles

duck

Bath time

plug

taps

bubble bath

saucepan

washing-up bowl

oven gloves

microwave

chopping board

Dinner time

cheese

jug

potato

fish

glass

broccoli

climbing frame

hide and seek

trampoline

sandpit

butterfly

tree

squirrel

beetle

leaf

logs

bee

flowers

frog

In the garden

ladybird

bird

pond

pasta

bread

salad

lettuce

carrot

kettle

yogurt

apple

cucumber

tomato

banana

sandwich

pan

toaster

plate

knife fork

ketchup

Making lunch

tins

bags

till

trolley

At the market

fruit

cake

bread

vegetables

scooter

bench

rollerskates

dog

cat

In the park

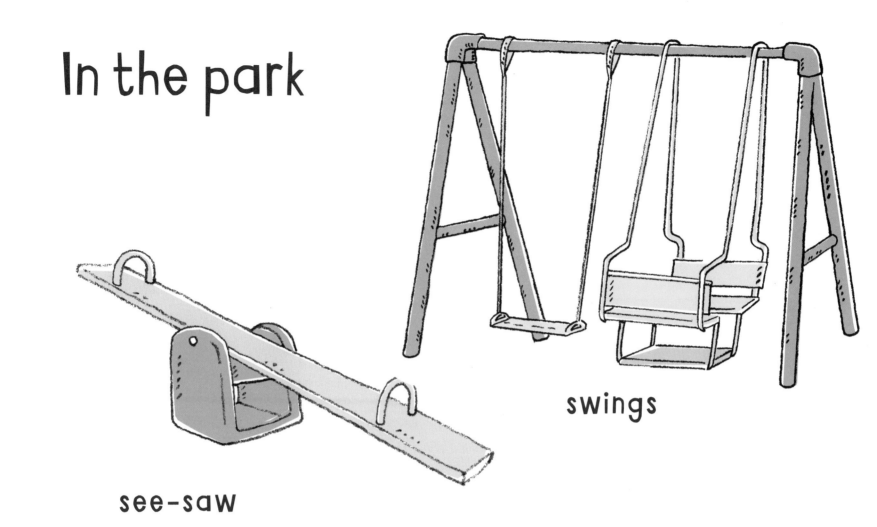

swings

see-saw

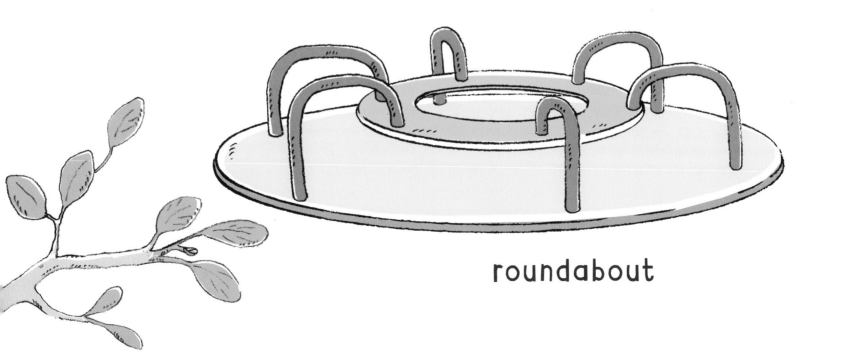

roundabout

roof

sun

door

window

tree

bicycle

waste bin

lamp post

Along the street

shop

car

buggy

music time

blowing bubbles

In the kitchen

painting

baking biscuits

drawing

dressing up

books

Let's play

trains

trousers

pants

nappy   T-shirt

Getting dressed

shorts

cardigan

vest

socks

brushing teeth

brushing hair

Toilet and teeth

Toilet paper

towel

sink

potty

soap

toothpaste

toothbrush

cotton wool

comb

hairbrush

mirror

spoon

butter

jam

cereal box

toast

bib

sippy cup

Eating breakfast

cup

bowl

milk

juice

egg

mug

bottle

pillows

blankets

quilt

rabbit

teddy

sun

window

clouds

clock

slippers

sleepsuit

nightie

dressing gown

pyjamas

Waking up

bunk beds

cot

My Day
FIRST WORDS

HIGH LIFE HIGHLAND LIBRARIES	
38001600859551	
BERTRAMS	14/03/2017
	£9.99
JF	

Illustrated by Marilyn Janovitz

BLOOMSBURY
LONDON OXFORD NEW YORK NEW DELHI SYDNEY

D0410381